LOOKIN

Looking Back

Fleur Adcock

Oxford   New York   Auckland

OXFORD UNIVERSITY PRESS

1997

Oxford University Press, Great Clarendon Street, Oxford OX2 6DP

Oxford New York
Athens Auckland Bangkok Bogota Bombay Buenos Aires
Calcutta Cape Town Dar es Salaam Delhi Florence Hong Kong Istanbul
Karachi Kuala Lumpur Madras Madrid Melbourne Mexico City
Nairobi Paris Singapore Taipei Tokyo Toronto Warsaw
and associated companies in
Berlin Ibadan

Oxford is a trade mark of Oxford University Press

First published in Oxford Poets as an Oxford University Press paperback 1997

British Library Cataloguing in Publication Data
Data available

Library of Congress Cataloguing in Publication Data
Data available
ISBN 0-19-288068-3

10 9 8 7 6 5 4 3 2 1

Typset by Rowland Phototypesetting Limited
Printed in Hong Kong

For my sister Marilyn

ACKNOWLEDGEMENTS

Acknowledgements are due to the editors of the following
publications in which some of these poems first appeared:
*ABSA Annual Report, 1990, The Honest Ulsterman, The
Independent, The London Review of Books, The New Welsh Review,
New Writing 5, New Zealand Books, Orbis, PN Review, Poetry Book
Society Anthologies, Poetry Review, Poetry Wales, The Rialto, Soho
Square, Stand, Stet, The Sunday Times, Thumbscrew, Verse, Voices
(Australia).* Poems have also appeared in the student magazines
of the Norwich School of Art, Queen's University Belfast, and
the University of East Anglia.

CONTENTS

I

WHERE THEY LIVED

That's where they lived in the 1890s.
They don't know that we know,
or that we're standing here, in possession
of some really quite intimate information
about the causes of their deaths,
photographing each other in a brisk wind
outside their terrace house, both smiling
(not callously, we could assure them),
our hair streaming across our faces
and the green plastic Marks and Spencer's bag
in which I wrapped my camera against showers
ballooning out like a wind-sock
from my wrist, showing the direction
of something that's blowing down our century.

FRAMED

(Sam Adcock, 1876–1956, and Eva Eggington, 1875–1970)

What shall we do with Grandpa, in his silver
frame? And why is he in it, may we ask?
Why not Grandma, still shyly veiled in her
tissue paper and photographer's cardboard?

Of course, there's his moustache: we can't miss that;
nor would he wish us to. It must have taken
hours and all his barbering skills to wax
and twirl the ends into these solemn curlicues.

We can't keep that in a drawer—or he couldn't.
But Grandma, now, in her black, nervously smiling,
one hand barely poised on the same ridiculous
Empire chairback: what a stunner she was!

Why did he not frame her? After all, her looks
are what he married her for. He fell in love
with her portrait (not this one) in a photographer's
window, and hunted down the woman herself.

She was a dressmaker's cutter (cool hands);
he was an extrovert—a talker, mixer
(the Lodge, the Church, the Mechanics' Institute,
the Temperance Movement). And it all came true:

seven years of engagement, fifty more
together. You can almost map their marriage,
decade by decade, through the evolution,
flourishing and decline of his moustache.

At twenty, not a whisker; at thirty or so,
this elaborate facial construct. In Manchester
it throve; then what did he do but export it
to droop and sag in the bush at Te Raua Moa,

on his dairy farm (how those cattle depressed him—
was New Zealand not such a bright idea after all?)
But it perked up for his passport in the '30s,
with a devilish Vandyke beard, for their last trip Home.

Not a handsome man, he must have decided
to take a bit of trouble and pass for one;
while Grandma, with the eyes and the bone structure
and that tilt of the head, decided to be plain.

She took to bobbed hair and wire-framed glasses,
and went grey early. He never did (unless
there was some preparation he knew about?)
Here they are in a '50s Polyfoto—

she with her shy smile, he with a muted version
of the moustache, wearing his cameo tie-pin
and a jubilant grin, as if he'd just slammed down
the winning trick in his favourite game of 'Sorry!'

THE RUSSIAN WAR

Great-great-great-uncle Francis Eggington
came back from the Russian War
(it was the kind of war you came back from,
if you were lucky: bad, but over).
He didn't come to the front door—
the lice and filth were falling off him—
he slipped along the alley to the yard.
'Who's that out at the pump?' they said
'—a tall tramp stripping his rags off!'
The soap was where it usually was.
He scrubbed and splashed and scrubbed,
and combed his beard over the hole in his throat.
'Give me some clothes' he said. 'I'm back.'
'God save us, Frank, it's you!' they said.
'What happened? Were you at Scutari?
And what's that hole inside your beard?'
'Tea first' he said. 'I'll tell you later.
And Willie's children will tell their grandchildren;
I'll be a thing called oral history.'

Failing their flesh and bones we have the gatepost.
Failing the bride in her ostrich-feathered hat,
the groom bracing his shoulders for the camera,
we have the garden wall, the path, and the gatepost:

not the original gatepost, but positioned
in exactly the same relation to the house—
just as the windows have been modernised
but we can see their dimensions are the same

as the ones behind the handsome brothers' heads
under their wedding bowlers. The gatepost
stands to the left, where nine-year-old Nellie
ought to be standing, in her home-made dress,

her boots and stockings and white hair-ribbon,
leaning her wistful head against Marion—
her next-best sister, who will have to do
now that Eva's married and going away.

Father and Mother, corpulent on chairs,
young Harry wincing in his Fauntleroy collar,
James in his first hard hat, a size too large,
have faded away from bricks and wood and metal.

Failing the sight of Mary, flowered and frilled,
the married sister, simpering on the arm
of Abraham with his curled moustache (the swine:
he'll leave her, of course) we may inspect the drainpipe:

not the authentic late-Victorian drainpipe
but just where that one was, convincing proof
(together with the gatepost and the windows)
that this is it, all right: the very house—

unless it's not; unless that was a stand-in,
one the photographer preferred that day
and lined them up in front of, because the sun
was shining on it; as it isn't now.

NELLIE

(*i.m. Nellie Eggington, 1894–1913*)

Just because it was so long ago
doesn't mean it ceases to be sad.
Nellie on the sea-front at Torquay
watching the fishing-boats ('Dear Sis and Bro,
I am feeling very much better') had
six months left to die of her TB.

She and Marion caught it at the mill
from a girl who coughed and coughed across her loom.
Their father caught it; he and Marion died;
the others quaked and murmured; James fell ill.
So here was Nellie, with her rented room,
carefully walking down to watch the tide.

When she'd first been diagnosed, she'd said
'Please, could Eva nurse me, later on,
when it's time, that is . . . if I get worse?'
Eva swallowed hard and shook her head
(and grieved for fifty years): she had her son
to consider. So their mother went as nurse.

Nellie took her parrot to Torquay—
her pet (as she herself had been a pet,
Eva's and her father's); she could teach
words to it in the evenings after tea,
talk to it when the weather was too wet
or she too frail for sitting on the beach.

Back in Manchester they had to wait,
looking out for letters every day,
or postcards for 'Dear Sis'. The winter passed.
Eva and Sam made plans to emigrate.
(Not yet, though. Later.) April came, and May—
bringing something from Torquay at last:

news. It was Tom's Alice who glanced out,
and called to Eva; Eva called to Sam:
'Look! Here's Mother walking up the road
with Nellie's parrot in its cage.' No doubt
now of what had happened. On she came,
steadily carrying her sharp-clawed load.

MARY DERRY

The first spring of the new century
and there I was, fallen pregnant!

Scarcely out of winter, even—
scarcely 1800 at all—

with not a bud on the trees yet
when the new thing budded in me.

They said I ought to have known better:
after all, I was over thirty.

William was younger; and men, of course . . .
but he came round fair in the end.

We couldn't sit the banns through,
giggled at for three Sundays—

not in Lichfield. He got a licence
and wedded me the next morning

in Armitage. July, it was
by then, and my loose gown bulging.

The babe was christened in Lichfield, though.
You knew he died? The wages of sin.

*

So this is where we began again:
Liverpool. Can you hear the seagulls?

A screeching city: seagulls and wagons,
drawbridges, floodgates, lifting-gear,

and warehouses huge as cathedrals.
We lived down by the Duke's Dock,

one lodging after another.
The family grew as the city grew.

William sat on his high stool
inscribing figures in a ledger.

My care was the children, bless them.
I ferried most of them safely through

the perilous waters of infancy,
and saw them married. Then I died.

*

Well, of course you know that.
And you know what of: consumption,

a word you don't use; an unwilled
legacy to go haunting down

one line of my long posterity
to Frank's son, and his son's son,

and fan out in a shuddering shadow
over the fourth generation.

And what I have to ask is:
was it the city's fault, or mine?

You can't answer me. All you hear
is a faint mewing among the seagulls.

MOSES LAMBERT: THE FACTS

The young cordwainer (yes, that's right)
got married at the Old Church—
it's Manchester Cathedral now.
That was the cheapest place to go.

They married you in batches there—
a list of names, a buzz of responses,
and 'You're all married' said the clerk.
'Pair up outside'. (Like shoes, thought Moses.)

After the ceremony, though,
he and Maria waited on.
They had an extra thing to do:
their daughter needed christening.

The baby's age is not recorded.
The bride was over twenty-one—
full age. The bridegroom (never mind
what he might have said) was seventeen.

The young Queen was on the throne;
they'd have to be Victorians now.
Meanwhile, two more facts: they were
from Leeds. One of them had red hair.

SAMUEL JOYNSON

He looked for it in the streets first,
and the sooty back alleys. It wasn't there.

He looked for it in the beer-house;
it dodged away as soon as he glimpsed it.

It certainly wasn't there at work,
raining down with the sawdust on to
his broad-brimmed hat as he stood sweating
in the pit under the snorting blade.

He looked all over the house for it—
the kitchen the scullery the parlour
the bedroom he shared with two of his brothers—
and shrugged. Of course it wasn't there.

So he tied a noose around where it should have been,
and slipped his head into it, for one last look.

AMELIA

It went like this: I married at 22,
in 1870. My daughter was born
the following year—Laura, we called her.
(No reason for the name—we just liked it.)
In '72 my brother hanged himself.
Laura died exactly a year later,
when I was pregnant with her brother Thomas
(named for my dead father). In '74
three things happened: my baby Thomas died,
then my sister; then I gave birth to John,
my first child to survive. He was a hunchback.
(I don't suppose you care for that expression;
well, call it what you like.) He lived to 20,
making the best of things, my poor brave lad.

After him, I got the knack of producing
healthy children. Or perhaps it was the gin.
Yes, I took to the bottle. Wouldn't you?
By the time it killed me I'd five living—
a little Band of Hope, a bright household
of teetotallers, my husband at their head.
I died of a stroke, officially; 'of drink'
wasn't spoken aloud for forty years.
These youngsters have my portrait proudly framed—
an old thing in a shawl, with a huge nose.
They also have a photograph—a maiden
with frightened eyes and a nose as trim as theirs.
Both are labelled 'Amelia'. Which one
was I? I couldn't have been both, they're sure.

BARBER

They set the boy to hairdressing—
you didn't need to be strong, or have
a straight back like other people.

It was the scissors he liked—their glitter
and snicker-snack; the arts, too,
of elegant shaping. Oh, and the razors.

He served his time, and qualified young;
it's on his death certificate:
'Hairdresser (Master). Age 20'.

In the next column, 'Spinal disease,
15 months. Abscess, 12 months'.
That sounds like cancer. It felt like blades

burning, slicing—a whole year
to play the Little Mermaid, walking
on knife-edges, with hand-glass and comb.

FLAMES

Which redhead did I get my temper from?
I've made a short ancestral list
by hair-colour and moods. But, more to the point,
what are the odds on Alzheimer's?

Which ones went funny in their seventies?
Mary Ellen, perhaps, found in the coal-shed
hunting for her Ship Canal shares
after her fiery hair turned grey.

My hair's not red. I like flames, though.
When I get old and mad I'll play with them —
run the flimsy veils through my fingers
like orange plastic film, like parachute-silk.

My hands will scorch and wither, if I do.
I shall be safe and dead. It won't matter.
It's something to look forward to,
playing with fire. That, or deep water.

WATER

I met an ancestor in the lane.
She couldn't stop: she was carrying water.
It slopped and bounced from the stoup against her;
the side of her skirt was dark with the stain,
oozing chillingly down to her shoe.
I stepped aside as she trudged past me,
frowning with effort, shivering slightly
(an icy drop splashed my foot too).
The dress that brushed against me was rough.
She didn't smell the way I smell:
I tasted the grease and smoke in her hair.
Water that's carried is never enough.
She'd a long haul back from the well.

No, I didn't see her. But she was there.

A HAUNTING

'Hoy!' A hand hooks me into a doorway:
'Here!' (No, that's not it: too many aitches;
they'd have been short of those, if I recall . . .)
'Oy, there!' (Never mind the aitches, it's his
breath now, gin and vinegar—I'm choking—
and fire on my neck; the hand grinding my shoulder.
I'm a head taller, nearly, but he's strong.)
'Look at me! I'm your ancestor.'

Eyes in a smudged face. Dark clothes. A hat . . .
'Look at me!' A stunted stump of a man.
Boots. No coat, although it's cold. A jacket
crumpled at the elbows. (I'm shivering.)
What kind of hair? If I can get
my hands to move, I'll push his hat off. There:
black, above a gleam of white skin (oh you poor
factory rat, you bastard you, my forebear!)

'Which one are you? Which ancestor?' Won't say.
Won't talk now. Stands there, shaking me now and then,
staring. Dark-haired—but then so were they all
in the photographs: brown hair, red hair, grey,
all dark for the cameras; and unsmiling.
This one's before photography,
still on the verge of things: a pre-Victorian,
pre-Temperance, pre-gentility; and angry.

He shows a snaggle of teeth (pre-dentistry);
means another thing now: 'Give us a kiss!'
No. No, I can't. 'Why not? You're family.'
That's not a family expression on his face.
'You're a woman, aren't you? One of ours?
A great-great-great-granddaughter?' He looks
younger than me, thirtyish. How do you talk
to a young man who's been dead a hundred years?

20

'Not unless you tell me who you are.'
'A part of you' he cackles. 'Never mind
which part.' (Is it compulsory, I wonder,
to like one's ancestors? I couldn't stand
that laugh of his for long.) 'You were so set
on digging us up. You thought it was romantic,
like all that poetry they talk about
(not me—I can't read.) Well, I'm what you dug.

So: what'll you give me for the favour, lass?
You wouldn't be on this earth if it weren't for me.'
That scorching gin-breath. 'Let me find my purse.'
We stagger together, a step or two, and I'm free.
His hat's on the cobbles. I rattle it full of money.
Not sovereigns, no: pound coins, worth less than a kiss—
base metal to him, proleptic wealth, no use
for more than a century to come. I'm sorry.

THE WARS

When they were having the Gulf War
I went to the 18th century.
I could see no glory in this life.

Awake half the night with the World Service,
then off on an early train for news—
secrets, discoveries, public knowledge

lurking on microfilm or parchment:
'I bequeath to my said daughter Mary Adcock
my Bedd and Bedding my oak Clothes Chest and Drawers

my Dressing Table and Looking Glass my Arm chair
my Clock standing in my said Dwelling house,
And one half part or share of all my Pewter.'

When it was over and not over,
and they offered us the Recession instead,
I went back further, pursuing the St Johns,

the Hampdens, the Wentworths to their deathbeds:
'Item I give to my wives sonne . . .'
(Ah, so she *had* been married before!)

'. . . Mr Edward Russell fiftie pounds,
and to John his brother ten pounds by the yeare
to be paid him soe long as he followes the warrs . . .'

SUB SEPIBUS

('*Many of this parish in the years ensuing were
marryed clandestinely, i.e.* sub sepibus, *and were
excommunicated for their labour.*' —
Note after entries for 1667 in Parish Register for
Syston, Leicestershire)

Under a hedge was good enough for us,
my Tommy Toon and me—
under the blackthorn, under the may,
under the stars at the end of the day,
under his cloak I lay,
under the shining changes of the moon;
under Tom Toon.

No banns or prayer-book for the likes of us,
my Tommy Toon and me.
Tom worked hard at his frame all day
but summer nights he'd come out to play,
in the hedge or the hay,
and ply his shuttle to a different tune—
my merry Tom Toon.

The vicar excommunicated us,
my Tommy Toon and me.
We weren't the only ones to stray—
there are plenty who lay down where we lay
and have babes on the way.
I'll see my tickling bellyful quite soon:
another Tom Toon.

ANNE WELBY

(*Died 9 May 1770, Beeby, Leicestershire*)

For her gravestone to have been moved is OK.
I know she isn't here, under the nettles;
but what did I want to do, after all—
burrow into the earth and stroke her skull?

Would that help me to see her? Would she rise
from the weeds ('Dormuit non mortua est')
and stand clutching at elder branches to prop
her dizzy bones after centuries of sleep?

The nettles, in fact, have also been removed:
a kind man with a spade has just slain them
so that I could kneel on the earth and scan
the truths, half-truths and guesses on her stone.

'Here lie the earthy remains' (I like 'earthy')
'of Ann the wife of Henry King'; then (huge
letters) 'Gentleman'. Not quite, I think:
it was his children who cried out their rank.

Henry was a grazier in his will;
but Anne, his lady, brought him eighty acres
and a fading touch of class; then lived so long
they buried a legend here—her age is wrong.

Homage (or weariness) called her 95,
adding perhaps five years. Her birth's gone under
the rubble of time, just as her grave was lost
when the church expanded a few yards to the east.

But I know who she was. I've traced her lineage
through wills and marriage bonds until I know it
better than she herself may have done, poor dear,
having outlived her age. And yes, she's here:

I've brought her with me. As I stroke the stone
with hands related to hers, I can feel
the charge transmitted through eight steps
of generations. She's at my finger-tips.

BEANFIELD

Somehow you've driven fifty miles to stand
in a beanfield, on the bumpy ridges
at the edge of it, not among the blossom
but under the larks—you can hear but not see them;
and it's not even where the house was—
the house, you think, was under the airfield
(beanfield, airfield, ploughed field)—
they ploughed the house but left the twitter of larks,
a pins-and-needles aerial tingling;
yet somehow this, you're sure, is Frances St John.
How do you know? It just is.
She's here; she's not here; she was once.
The larks are other larks' descendants.
Four hundred years. It feels like a kind of love.

ANCESTOR TO DEVOTEE

What are you loving me with? I'm dead.
What gland of tenderness throbs in you,
yearning back through the silt of ages
to a face and a voice you never knew?

When you find my name in a document
or my signature on a will,
what is it that makes you hold your breath—
what reverent, half-perverted thrill?

'Flesh of my flesh', we could call each other;
but not uniquely: I've hundreds more
in my posterity, and for you
unreckoned thousands have gone before.

What's left of me, if you gathered it up,
is a faggot of bones, some ink-scrawled paper,
flown-away cells of skin and hai r . . .
you could set the lot on fire with a taper.

You breathe your scorching filial love
on a web of related facts and a name.
But I'm combustible now. Watch out:
you'll burn me up with that blow-torch flame.

FRANCES

Her very hand. Her signature—
upright, spiky, jagged with effort—
or his hand on hers, was it,
her son's grasp locked on her knuckles?

'F. Weale'. Third of her surnames.
I Frances Weale of Arlesey,
widowe, being weake in body
but of perfecte memory,

doe make this my last will
in the yeare 1638 . . .
Item I give to my sonne Samuell Browne
my halfe dozen of silver spoones . . .

*

They've had quite a history, those spoons.
My first husband bequeathed them to my second—
or at least to his mother, Goodwife Weale:
'one haulfe dozen of silver spoones
which are alone and seldom occupied'—
little guessing they'd come back to me.

I was supposed to go away quietly
and live at Ashby Mill in Lincolnshire,
there to 'rest myself contented' and not
(repeat *not*—he did go on about it)
sue for my thirds, my widow's right in law.
Nicholas wasn't one for women's rights.

I was to have the bringing up of Samuel,
our older son; but John, our younger boy,
was to stay behind with the man Nicholas called
his 'trustie frende', Thomas Weale of Polebrook,
his joint executor. I was to be the other—
as long as I didn't claim my thirds, of course.

I was to keep the buildings in repair;
I wasn't to fell any of the trees . . .
he was going to rule us all from beyond the grave,
my iron rod of a husband, Nicholas Browne,
BA, BD, Rector of Polebrook, Prebendary
of Peterborough Cathedral; puritan.

Well, I wouldn't be ruled. I was done with that.
I'd had eleven years of being meek.
So when he tried to shunt me off up north
to the dull retreat he'd set aside for me
(such a fiddly, scholar's will), I didn't go.
I stayed at home and married Thomas Weale.

Yes, I know I was taking another master,
but this time I was doing it by choice;
and believe me if I tell you he was different—
a yeoman, not a cleric; less cold;
and, above all, my little John's guardian.
By marrying Thomas I kept both my children.

We made an execution of the will
to our joint satisfaction, I and Thomas
(I was still young, remember). We did our duties—
to Nicholas's estate, and to the boys
(we had no other children), and to each other.
Thomas Weale was a 'trustie frende' to us all.

No nagging about thirds when his time came:
he left me both his houses, and some land
(for my life-time only—but even a man, I think,
needs little land when he's dead), and his goods and plate.
Of which to my son John my silver bowl,
to his wife my silver cup; and the spoons to Samuel.

In witnes whereof I have set to
my hande the day & yeare above written . . .

                 *

F. Weale. Her final signature.
Her own fingers twitching across
this very page. Not John's hand—
he wasn't there. Not clever Samuel's—

his legal glibness would have made
a brisker job of it. The wobbling
jabs of the quill are hers, an image
of weakness spelling out her strength.

AT GREAT HAMPDEN

That can't be it—
not with cherubs.
After all, they were Puritans.

All the ones on the walls are too late—
too curlicued, ornate, rococo—
17th century at least.

Well, then, says the vicar,
it will be under the carpets:
a brass.

He strips off his surplice,
then his cassock,
hardly ruffling his white hair.

He rolls the strip of red carpet;
I roll the underfelt.
It sheds fluff.

A brass with figures appears. Not them.
Another. Not them.
We've begun at the wrong end.

Room for one more? Yes.
There, just in front of the altar,
a chaste plaque and a chaste coat of arms.

It says what the book says:
'Here lieth the body of Griffith Hampde n . . .
and of Ann . . .' No need to write it down.

Now we begin again, the vicar and I,
rolling the carpet back,
our heads bent to the ritual;

tweaking and tidying the heavy edges
we move our arms in reciprocal gestures
like women folding sheets in a launderette.

A button flips off someone's jacket.
Yours? I offer it to the vicar.
No, yours. He hands it back with a bow.

AT BADDESLEY CLINTON

A splodge of blood on the oak floor
in the upstairs parlour, near the hearth.

Nicholas Brome splashed it here
five centuries ago, the villain.

Not his blood; he kept his,
apart from what he handed down

(drops of it circulating still
in my own more law-abiding veins).

It was a priest's blood he squirted:
out with his sword and stuck it into

the local parson, whom he caught
'chockinge his wife under ye chinne'.

Not the same class of murder
as when he ambushed his father's killer.

That was cold blood at the crossroads;
hot blood in the parlour's different.

But he got the King's and the Pope's pardons,
and built the church a new west tower.

There it stands among the bluebells:
'NICHOLAS BROME ESQVIRE LORD OF

BADDESLEY DID NEW BVILD THIS STEEPLE
IN THE RAIGNE OF KING HENRY THE SEAVENTH.'

His other memorial was more furtive;
it trickled down under the rushes

and stayed there. Easy to cover it up,
but more fun now for the tourists

to see it crying out his crime.
It *is* blood: they've analysed it.

On some surfaces, in some textures,
blood's indelible, they say.

TRAITORS

'... *For that preposterous sinne wherein he did offend,*
In his posteriour parts had his preposterous end.'
~~Michael~~ Drayton: *Poly-Olbion* (on Edward II,
murdered by Roger de Mortimer, 1327)

Naughty ancestors, I tell them,
baby-talking my cosy family—
the history ones, the long-ago
cut-out figures I've found in books.

Cut up, too, a few of them: quartered—
you, for instance, regicide
who cuddled a king's wife, and then
had her husband done away with.

You never touched him yourself, of course;
but wasn't it your own vision,
to roger him to death like that,
a red-hot poker up his rear?

Well, he had it coming to him,
you might have sneered (I see you sneering:
a straight man, in that you preferred
women to Eddy-Teddy-bears).

It's never only about sex.
Power, as usual, was the hormone;
and two of those who had the power
were my other naughties, the Despensers.

It wasn't Hugh the king's playmate
but Hugh his father who begat us,
through a less blatant son. Both Hughs
lost their balls before the scaffold.

That was how the sequence went,
for treason: chop, then hang, then quarter.
So fell all three. Only the king
died without a mark on his body—

or so they say. It's all hearsay.
Perhaps the king and Hugh the younger
were just good friends; perhaps the murder
wasn't a murder; perhaps the blood

of traitors isn't in my veins,
but just the blood of ambitious crooks
with winning Anglo-Norman accents
and risky tastes in sex. Perhaps.

Blood must be in it somewhere, though;
I see them bundled into a box,
dismembered toys, still faintly squeaking,
one with royal blood on his paws.

SWINGS AND ROUNDABOUTS

My ancestors are creeping down from the north—
from Lancashire and the West Riding,
from sites all over Leicestershire,

down through the Midlands; from their solid outpost
in Lincolnshire, and their halts in Rutland,
down through Northants and Beds and Bucks.

They're doing it backwards, through the centuries:
from the Industrial Revolution
they're heading south, past the Enclosures

and the Civil War, through Elizabethan times
to the dissolution of the monasteries,
the Wars of the Roses, and beyond.

From back-to-backs in Manchester they glide
in reverse to stocking-frames in Syston,
from there back to their little farms,

then further back to grander premises,
acquiring coats of arms and schooling
in their regression to higher things.

They're using the motorways; they're driving south
in their armour or their ruffs and doublets
along the M1 and the A1.

They've got as far as the South Mimms roundabout.
A little group in merchants' robes
is filtering through London, aiming

for a manor-house and lands in Chislehurst
across the road from a school I went to;
and somewhere round about Footscray

they'll meet me riding my bike with Lizzie Wood
when I was twelve; they'll rush right through me
and blow the lot of us back to Domesday.

PETER WENTWORTH IN HEAVEN

The trees have all gone from the grounds of my manor—
the plums, quinces, close-leaved pears—
where I walked in the orchard, planning my great speech;
and the house gone too. No matter.

My *Pithie Exhortation* still exists—
go and read it in your British Library.
I have discussed it here with your father;
he was always a supporter of free speech.

The trouble it brought me it is not in my nature
to regret. Only for my wife I grieved:
she followed me faithfully into the Tower;
her bones lie there, in St Peter ad Vincula.

I would not have gone home to Lillingstone Lovell,
if my friends had gained my release, without her,
'my chiefest comfort in this life, even
the best wife that ever poor gentleman enjoyed'.

She was a Walsingham; her subtle brother
was the Queen's man; he guarded his own back.
Any fellow-feeling he may once have cherished
for our cause he strangled in his bosom.

I was too fiery a Puritan for him.
His wife remembered mine in her will:
'to my sister Wentworthe a payre of sables'.
Not so Francis: he was no brother to us.

Well, we are translated to a different life,
my loyal Elizabeth and I.
We walk together in the orchards of Heaven—
a place I think you might find surprising.

But then you found me surprising too
when you got some notion of me, out of books.
Read my *Exhortation*, and my *Discourse*;
so you may understand me when we come to meet.

II

TONGUE SANDWICHES

Tongue sandwiches on market-day
in the King's Head Hottle (I could read;
my sister couldn't.) Always the same
for lunch on market-day in Melton.

No sign of a bottle in the hottle—
or not upstairs in the dining-room;
the bottles were in the room below,
with the jolly farmers around the door.

I didn't know we were in a pub,
or quite what pubs were: Uncle managed
to be a not unjolly farmer
with only tea to loosen his tongue.

And what did I think 'tongue' was?
These rose-pink slices wrapped in bread?
Or the slithery-flappy tube behind
my milk-teeth, lapping at novelties

(yes, of course I'd heard of 'ho-*tells*')
and syphoning up Midlands vowels
to smother my colonial whine?
(Something new for Mummy and Daddy,

coming to visit us at Christmas,
these local 'oohs' and 'ahs', as in
'Moommy, there's blood in the lavatory!
Soombody moost have killed a rabbit.')

On the way back to Uncle's cart
(how neat that his name was George Carter!)
we passed the beasts in the cattle-stalls—
their drooling lips, their slathering tongues.

The horse was a safer kind of monster,
elephant-calm between the shafts
as Auntie and Uncle loaded up
and we all piled on. Then bumpety-bump

along the lanes. I was impatient
for *Jerry of St Winifred's*—
my Sunday School prize, my first real book
that wasn't babyish with pictures—

to curl up with it in the armchair
beside the range, for my evening ration:
'Only a chapter a day', said Auntie.
'Too much reading's bad for your eyes.'

I stuck my tongue out (not at her—
in a trance of concentration), tasting
the thrilling syllables: 'veterinary
surgeon', 'papyrus', 'manuscript'.

Jerry was going to be a vet;
so when she found the injured puppy
and bandaged its paw with her handkerchief,
and the Squire thanked her—well, you could see!

As for me, when I sat for hours
writing a story for Mummy and Daddy,
and folded the pages down the middle
to make a book, I had no ambition.

THE PILGRIM FATHERS

I got a Gold Star for the Pilgrim Fathers,
my first public poem, when I was nine.
I think I had to read it out to the class;
but no one grilled me about it, line by line;

no one asked me to expatiate on
my reasons for employing a refrain;
no one probed into my influences,
or said 'Miss Adcock, perhaps you could explain

your position as regards colonialism.
Here you are, a New Zealander in Surrey,
describing the exportation of new values
to America. Does this cause you any worry?

And what about the title, "Pilgrim Fathers"—
a patriarchal expression, you'll agree—
how does it relate to the crucial sentence
in stanza one: "Nine children sailed with we"?

Were you identifying with your age-group?
Some of us have wondered if we detect
a growing tendency to childism
in your recent poems. Might this be correct?'

No one even commented on the grammar—
it didn't seem important at the time.
I liked the sound of it, is all I'd have said
if they'd questioned me. I did it for the rhyme.

PAREMATA

Light the Tilley lamp:
I want to write a message,
while the tide laps the slipway
and someone else cooks sausages.

Make the Primus hiss:
twizzley music. Dusk time.
Bring back the greeds of childhood;
forget young love and all that slime.

CAMPING

When you're fifteen, no one understands you.
And why had I been invited, anyway?—
On a camping holiday with my Latin teacher
and her young friends, two men in their twenties.
I didn't understand them, either.

The one I fancied was the tall one
with soft brown eyes. He was a hairdresser.
One day the primus toppled over
and a pan of water scalded his foot.
The skin turned into soggy pink crepe paper—
grisly; but it gave him a romantic limp
and a lot of sympathy.
Once he condescended to lean on my shoulder
for a few steps along a wooded path.
Next time I offered, he just laughed.

Funnily enough, two days later
I scalded my own foot: not badly,
but as badly as I dared.
                           It didn't work.
Everyone understood me perfectly.

BED AND BREAKFAST

They thought he looked like Gregory Peck, of course;
and they thought I looked like Anne somebody—
a name I vaguely recognised: no one special,
not Greer Garson or Vivien Leigh.
What they really must have thought I looked like
was young. But they were being kind;
and anyway, we'd asked for separate rooms.

When it was late enough, Gregory Peck
came into mine—or did I go into his?
Which of us tiptoed along the passage
in our pyjamas? And to do what?
                                   Not sex,
but what you did when you weren't quite doing sex.
It made you a bit sticky and sweaty,
but it didn't make you pregnant,
and you didn't actually have to know anything.
You didn't even take off your pyjamas.

Unfortunately since it never got anywhere
it went on most of the night. No sleep.
At breakfast, though, I can't have looked too haggard:
Gregory Peck was not put off.
For that I could thank the resilience of youth—
one of the very few advantages,
as far as I could see, of that hateful condition.
Anne Whatsit might have looked worse;
but then I suppose she'd have had makeup.

RATS

That was the year the rats got in:
always somebody at the back door
clutching a half-dozen of beer,
asking if we felt like a game of darts.

Then eyes flickering away from the dartboard
to needle it out. What were we up to?
Were we really all living together—
three of us? Four of us? Who was whose?

And what about the children? What indeed.
We found a real rat once, dead
on the wash-house floor. Not poison:
old age, perhaps, or our old cat.

We buried the corpse. Our own victims
were only our reputations, we thought—
bright-eyed with panic and bravado.
It can take thirty years to find out.

STOCKINGS

The first transvestite I ever went to bed with
was the last, as far as I know.
It was in the 60s, just before tights.
He asked if he could put my stockings on—
on me, I thought; on him, it turned out.
His legs weren't much of a shape,
and my suspender-belt was never the same
after he'd strained it round his middle.
But apart from that, things could have been worse.
The whisky helped.

I never went out with him again;
and I never, ever, told his secret—
who'd want to? (He must have counted on
the inhibiting power of embarrassment.)
But I still went to his parties.
At one of them I met Yoko Ono.

A POLITICAL KISS

In the dream I was kissing John Prescott—
or about to kiss him; our eyes had locked
and we were leaning avidly forward,
lips out-thrust, certain protuberances
under our clothing brushing each other's fronts,
when my mother saw us, and I woke up.

In fact I've never kissed an MP.
The nearest I got was a Labour peer
in a telephone box at Euston station
(one of the old red kiosks—
which seemed appropriate at the time).
But I don't suppose that counts, does it?

AN APOLOGY

Can it be that I was unfair
to Tony Blair?
His teeth, after all, are beyond compare;
but does he take too much care
over his hair?

If he were to ask me out for a meal,
how would I feel?
Would I grovel and kneel,
aflame with atavistic socialist zeal?
No, I'm sorry, he doesn't appeal:
he's not quite real.

In the House he sounds sincere,
but over a candlelit table, I fear,
his accents wouldn't ring sweetly in my ear.
Oh dear.

I'd love to see him in No. 10,
but he doesn't match my taste in men.

FESTSCHRIFT

Dear So-and-so, you're seventy. Well done!
Or is it sixty? It's a bit confusing
remembering which, of all my ageing friends,
is the one about whose talents I'm enthusing.

I'm getting on myself, a fact which makes one
occasionally vague—as you may know,
having achieved such venerable status;
although in you, of course, the years don't show.

Anyway, I'm delighted to contribute
to the memorial volume which your wife—
or publisher—is secretly arranging
to mark this splendid milestone in your life.

As one of your most passionate admirers
I'm glad to tell the world of my conviction
that you've transformed the course of literature
by your poetry—or do I mean your fiction?

Oh dear. Well, never mind. Congratulations,
from a near contemporary, on your weighty
achievements; and you'll hear this all again
in ten years' time, at seventy—sorry!—eighty.

OFFERINGS

A garland for Dame Propinquity, goddess
of work-places, closed circles and small towns,
who let our paths cross and our eyes meet
so many times in the course of duty
that we became each other's pleasure, and every
humdrum encounter a thundering in the veins.
We place at the hem of her fluted marble robe
this swag of meadow flowers, picked nearby,
as much a bribe as a thank-offering,
asking her to smile on our extensions
and elaborations of what she began.

And now, to be on the safe side, a recherché
confection of orchids and newly hybridized lilies
for her sister, Lady Novelty: not to leave us.

DANGER: SWIMMING AND BOATING PROHIBITED

This tender 'V' of thighs below my window
is one end of Kuba's mother,
sprawled for the May sun in her bikini.
I hardly know her face. 'Ku-baah!' she calls,
and scolds him drowsily in Polish.

Kuba's off with his bikie friends,
the big boys, old enough for school.
'Ku-baah!' they shout. Their accent's perfect.
They bump their tyres in circles over the grass,
towards and then away from the glinting water.

In winter, I'm told, the swans come up
and tap their beaks on the windows, begging.
Today a lone brown female mallard
waddles quacking forlorn parodies
of a person doing duck imitations.

Kuba tries to run her down.
She flaps off, squawking, back to the Broad.
It's a rough male world down there;
the drakes are playing football hooligans,
dunking each other, shamming rape—

well, what else is there to do
while their sober mates are hatching eggs?
Only one brood's appeared so far.
I count the ducklings every day:
eight, five, four, still four (good!), three . . .

I'll go and check again in a minute.
'Grow up!' I'll tell them. 'Hang on in there!'
Downstairs the front end of Kuba's mother,
a streaked blonde top-knot, pokes out of a window.
'Kuba!' she calls again. 'Ku-baah!'

RISKS

When we heard the results of our tests
we felt rather smug (if worried);
we said to each other loudly in public
'Well, that's it for space-travel;
we mustn't go up there again.
We can't afford to be bombarded
with any more radiation, dammit!'

No more risks: that was the policy.
In which case what are we doing here
scrambling along this rocky gorge
with hardly a finger-hold to bless us,
and the bridge down, and a train coming,
and the river full of crocodiles?
(I think I invented the crocodiles.)

BLUE FOOTPRINTS IN THE SNOW

But there's no snow yet: the footprints
are made by a rubber stamp, a toy
I daren't give to a child. (Warning:
'Ink not guaranteed to wash out.')

First the gale, and now the rain,
and soon the sleet, and then the footprints.

The TV weather map is stamped
with rows of identical cloud-shapes,
each dangling two white crystals
and striding briskly south from Scotland.

But the feet are close together, jumping
kangaroo-hops on a white page.

We thought we were stuck on Crusoe's island,
marooned in summer, dry and stranded
under clouds that would come to nothing—
or nothing anyone could want.

Earth-based, earth-bound, paper-bound,
we had to play with toy footprints.

Now, though, prophetic silhouettes
emerge from a computer to bless us.
The clouds leap up; the crystals fall
and multiply on roofs and gardens.

The feet are lifting off the page
to bite blue shadows into the snow.

SUMMER IN BUCHAREST

We bought raspberries in the market;
but raspberries are discredited:

they sag in their bag, fermenting
into a froth of suspect juice.

And strawberries are seriously compromised:
a taint—you must have heard the stories.

As for red currants, well, they say
the only real red currants are dead.

(Don't you believe it: the fields are full of them,
swelling hopefully on their twigs,

and the dead ones weren't red anyway
but some mutation of black or white.)

We thought of choosing gooseberries,
until we heard they'd been infiltrated

by raspberries in gooseberry jackets.
You can't tell what to trust these days.

There are dates, they say, but they're imported;
and it's still too early for the grape harvest.

All we can do is wait and hope.
It's been a sour season for fruit.

1990

59

MONEYMORE

Looked better last time, somehow, on a wet weekday
from under an umbrella—rain
blurring my lens and rinsing the handsome faces
of the Drapers' Company buildings, lights on early,
golden glimmers in puddles, cars growling
at each other over parking spaces—

than on this mild and spacious Sunday afternoon,
no car but ours parked in the High Street
by the painted kerbstones—white, blue, red, white, blue,
with lads loafing in front of the Orange Hall
and an old woman, daft in the sunshine,
greeting strangers: 'How *are* you? How are *you*?'

Oh, yes, and that parked van outside the Market House . . .
but time's up; I've a plane to catch.
If we take the Ballyronan road
we shan't see Magherafelt, a town I've always
wanted to visit; where ten hours from now
another van will discharge its sudden load.

THE VOICES

The voices change on the answering-machines:
not the friend but the friend's widow;
not the friend but the other friend.

'I'm not here' the machine tells you.
'This is the job I never did—
this fluent interface with the world.

He/she did it; but I'm learning.
Now all the jobs are mine or no one's.
There's no one here. Leave a message.'

WILLOW CREEK

The janitor came out of his eely cave
and said 'Your mother was a good swimmer.
Go back and tell her it's not yet time.'

Were there no other animals in Eden?
When she dives under the roots, I thought,
an eel is the last shape she'll want to meet.

Her brother was the one for eels: farm-wise,
ruthless abut food. You roll the skin back
and pull it off inside out like a stocking.

He grew up with dogs, horses and cattle.
She was more at home with water and music;
there were several lives for her after the creek.

In one of them she taught my younger son
to swim in the Greek sea; and walked through Athens
under a parasol, to buy us melon.

Fruit for the grandchildren; nectarines and pears
for the great-grandchildren; feijoa-parties . . .
'There's more of that to come', said the janitor.

'But no more swimming. Remember how she plunged
into a hotel pool in bra and knickers,
rather than miss the chance? She must have been sixty.'

I had some questions for the janitor,
but he submerged himself under the willows
in his cavern where I couldn't follow—

you have to be invited; I wasn't, yet,
and neither was she. Meanwhile, she's been allowed
a rounded segment of something warm and golden:

not pomegranate, paw-paw. She used to advise
eating the seeds: a few of them, with the fruit,
were good for you in some way—I forget.

Long life, perhaps. She knows about these things.
And she won't let a few eels bother her.
She's tougher than you might think, my mother.

GIGGLING

I mustn't mention the hamster's nose—
it sets you off. You giggle like Auntie Lizzie
forty-odd years old, when she was your age:
heading for ninety. Great gigglers,
you and your mother and your aunt.
They were white-haired and well-padded;
you were too skinny for a mother,
we thought, with our teenage angst,
afraid of turning into you.

'It just struck me funny' said Auntie Lizzie
'—that old drunk in his coffin
with all those flowers. I got the giggles.'
Her comfortable shoulders heaved
as yours do, now that you're her shape.
She lived to a hundred and three,
blind and deaf at the end, but not to be fooled:
when her daughter died, she knew.
I hope you'll be spared that extremity.

Of course it wasn't the hamster's nose:
that's just shorthand. It was the fireman's;
he'd given it the kiss of life,
and the hamster . . . oh, well, never mind—
you know the story. You're off again.
I never guessed old age was so much fun.

TRIO

Julia has chocolate on her chin,
and isn't getting far with the cut-out stick
they've given her as a bow. It doesn't matter;
the music's there, behind her serious eyes.

Lily's in her knickers and a sweater
passed down from Oliver, who hated it,
her shiny hair glinting above her shiny
half-sized (or is it quarter-sized?) violin.

Oliver's playing his cello: he knows how;
and that's not all he knows about: he made
the cardboard fiddle—bridge and strings and struts
and curves, a three-dimensional miracle

of Sellotaping—for Julia to play at
playing like Lily, and for family harmony.
Soon, after her birthday, when she's four,
she'll have Suzuki lessons and the real thing.

THE VIDEO

When Laura was born, Ceri watched.
They all gathered around Mum's bed—
Dad and the midwife and Mum's sister
and Ceri. 'Move over a bit,' Dad said—
he was trying to focus the camcorder
on Mum's legs and the baby's head.

After she had a little sister,
and Mum had gone back to being thin,
and was twice as busy, Ceri played
the video again and again.
She watched Laura come out, and then,
in reverse, she made her go back in.

NOTES

p. 11   *Mary Derry* married William Eggington in 1800 and was the great-great-grandmother of Samuel Adcock's wife Eva Eggington.

p. 14   *Moses Lambert: the facts*: Moses Lambert, 1821–1868, was the father of Mary Ellen Lambert (not the premarital baby in this poem but a later child), who married William Henry Eggington and was the mother of Eva.

p. 15   *Samuel Joynson* was Amelia Joynson's brother.

p. 16   *Amelia*: Amelia Joynson, 1847–1899, married John Adcock, 1842–1911, and was Samuel Adcock's mother.

p. 17   *Barber*: John Adcock, 1874–1895, was the son of John and Amelia, and brother of Sam Adcock.

p. 24   *Anne Welby* married Henry King, 1680–1756. Their granddaughter Elizabeth King married William Adcock, 1737–1814, Samuel Adcock's great-great-grandfather.

pp. 26, 28   *Beanfield* and *Frances*: Frances St John married Nicholas Browne, rector of Polebrook, Northants., in 1597, and was Anne Welby's great-great-grandmother.

p. 31   *At Great Hampden*: Griffith Hampden, 1543–1591, and his wife Anne Cave were the parents of Mary Hampden who married Walter Wentworth, son of Peter. Their daughter Mary Wentworth married John Browne; these were the great-grandparents of Anne Welby.

pp. 33, 35   *At Baddesley Clinton* and *Traitors*: These assorted villains figure in the family tree of Elizabeth Ferrers, mother of Griffith Hampden. Baddesley Clinton is in Warwickshire; the house belongs to the National Trust.

p. 39   *Peter Wentworth in Heaven*: Peter Wentworth, MP, 1524–1597, was imprisoned in the Tower of London several times by Elizabeth I for demanding that Parliament should be free to discuss the succession and other matters without interference. His wife Elizabeth Walsingham died in 1596 in the Tower. Her sister-in-law who mentioned Elizabeth in her will was Sir Francis Walsingham's first wife, Anne.

OXFORD POETS

Fleur Adcock

Moniza Alvi

Kamau Brathwaite

Joseph Brodsky

Basil Bunting

Tessa Rose Chester

Daniela Crăsnaru

Michael Donaghy

Keith Douglas

D. J. Enright

Roy Fisher

Ida Affleck Graves

Ivor Gurney

David Harsent

Gwen Harwood

Anthony Hecht

Zbigniew Herbert

Tobias Hill

Thomas Kinsella

Brad Leithauser

Derek Mahon

Jamie McKendrick

Sean O'Brien

Alice Oswald

Peter Porter

Craig Raine

Zsuzsa Rakovszky

Christopher Reid

Stephen Romer

Eva Salzman

Carole Satyamurti

Peter Scupham

Jo Shapcott

Penelope Shuttle

Goran Simić

Anne Stevenson

George Szirtes

Grete Tartler

Edward Thomas

Charles Tomlinson

Marina Tsvetaeva

Chris Wallace-Crabbe

Hugo Williams